Handy Oregon Genealogy Handbook

Gary L. Morris

©2015 Gary L. Morris

ISBN-13: 978-1507840511

ISBN-10: 1507840519

Table of Contents

Notes

Genealogical Research in Oregon

As one of the original "frontier" states, there are many genealogical records and resources available for tracing your family history in Oregon. Because there are so many records held at many different locations, tracking down the records for your ancestor can be an ominous task. Don't worry though, we know just where they are, and we'll show you which records you'll need, while helping you to understand:

1. What they are
2. Where to find them
3. How to use them

These records can be found both online and off, so we'll introduce you to online websites, indexes and databases, as well as brick-and-mortar repositories and other institutions that will help with your research in Oregon. So that you will have a more comprehensive understanding of these records, we have provided a brief history of the "Beaver State" to illustrate what type of records may have been generated during specific time periods. That information will assist you in pinpointing times and locations on which to focus the search for your Oregon ancestors and their records.

A Brief History of Oregon

It is thought that Sir Francis Drake was the first European to see
Oregon during a raid on the Spanish in 1578. For the following two
centuries the only European contact was occasional sightings of the
coast by mariners who considered the area to dangerous for landings.
In 1778 Captain James Cook, visited the Northwest and gave names
to several Oregon capes. American ships soon frequented the area
carrying merchants seeking sea otter and other firs. One of them, an
American merchant captain, Robert Gray, discovered the Columbia
River in 1792, eventually leading to the US claim to the Northwest.

The Lewis and Clark Expedition arrived in the area, spending the
winter there from 1805–06, while the first traders established an
outpost at the mouth of the Columbia River in 1811. The
unsuccessful venture was sold to the British in three years later, and
the next twenty years British agents of the North West Company in
conjunction with some of the original American traders explored the
area, mapping trails and establishing more trading posts.

Although the Americans and British had agreed to joint occupation
of the region, the Hudson Bay Company, which had merged with the
North West Company, exerted the most influence in the area.
Protestant missionaries were also a major influence in the area,
establishing missions which eventually served as bases for white
settlement. The first wagon trains of any consequence arrived via the
Oregon Trail in the early 1840,s, eventually establishing a
provisional government in 1843.

The provisional government ruled until 1849 when Oregon became a
territory. The original Oregon Territory included parts of Idaho,
Wyoming, and Montana, and all of present day Washington State. A
constitution was approved in November 1857, and after a delay
caused by North-South rivalries, Congress voted to make Oregon,
the 33rd state on 14 February 1859.

Important Dates in Oregon History

1811 – Trading Post established at mouth of Columbia River at Astoria

1818 – US and Britain agree to joint occupation

1840's – First Wagon Trains arrive

1841 – First court system, based on New York law organized

1843 – Laws of Oregon Territory adopted

1847 – Cayuse Indian War begins

1848 – Cayuse Indian War ends, Oregon organized as a territory

1857 – Constitution adopted

1859 – Statehood

1883 – Northern Pacific Railway reaches Oregon

Famous Battles Fought in Oregon

There were no Civil War or any other major war battles fought in Oregon. There were however several minor **Indian Wars**.

These battle accounts that exist can be very effective in uncovering the military records of your ancestor. They can tell you what regiments fought in which battles, and often include the names and ranks of many officers and enlisted men.

Indian Wars:
http://bluebook.state.or.us/cultural/history/history14.htm

Common Oregon Genealogical Issues and Resources to Overcome Them

Boundary Changes: Boundary changes are a common obstacle when researching Oregon ancestors. You could be searching for an ancestor's record in one county when in fact it is stored in a different one due to historical county boundary changes.

The **Atlas of Historical County Boundaries** can help you to overcome that problem. It provides a chronological listing of every boundary change that has occurred in the history of Oregon.

Atlas of Historical County Boundaries:
http://publications.newberry.org/ahcbp/documents/OR_Consolidated_Chronology.htm#Consolidated_Chronology

Name Changes: Surname changes, variations, and misspellings can complicate genealogical research. It is important to check all spelling variations. Soundex, a program that indexes names by sound, is a useful first step, but you can't rely on it completely as some name variations result in different Soundex codes. The surnames could be different, but the first name may be different too. You can also find records filed under initials, middle names, and nicknames as well, so you will need to **get creative with surname variations** and spellings in order to cover all the possibilities. For help with surname variations read our instructional article on **How to Use Soundex**.

get creative with surname variations:
http://obituarieshelp.org/blog/?p=634

How to Use Soundex: http://obituarieshelp.org/blog/?p=505

Oregon Genealogical Organizations and Archives

Genealogical resources include not only records, but the organizations that house them, or can direct you to them. These institutions include: *Archives, Libraries, Genealogical Societies, Family History Centers, Universities, Churches, and Museums.*

Following are links to their websites, their physical addresses, and a summary of the records you can find there.

Archives and Libraries

Oregon State Archives - Adoption records, Census records, Land records, Military records, Naturalization records, Probate records, Vital records

800 Summer St. NE
Salem OR 97310
Tel:503-373-0701
Fax 503-373-0953

Oregon State Archives:
http://sos.oregon.gov/archives/Pages/records.aspx

University of Oregon Libraries - Cemeteries, Regimental histories, Registers of births, Marriage records, Divorce records, Church records and registers, Naturalization records, Land grants , city directories, historical newspapers, and much more

1501 Kincaid Street,
Eugene, OR 97403-1299
Tel: (541) 346-3053
Fax: (541) 346-3485

University of Oregon Libraries:
http://library.uoregon.edu/guides/genealogy/index.html

National Archives—Pacific Alaska Region (Seattle) - Federal population censuses for all States, 1790-1930, military service records, pension and bounty land warrant applications, passenger arrival and naturalization records, records relating to the Five Civilized Tribes

6125 Sand Point Way, N.E.
Seattle, WA 98115-7999
Telephone: 206-336-5115
Fax: 206-336-5112

National Archives—Pacific Alaska Region (Seattle):
http://www.archives.gov/seattle/

Oregon Genealogical and Historical Societies

Genealogical and historical societies have access to extensive catalogues of genealogical data. They are also able to offer expert guidance for genealogical researchers. Many members are professional genealogists who are most willing to share their expertise in finding ancestors.

The Oregon Historical Society – census records, city directories, Indian Wars Pensions Index, DAR Index, manuscripts, historical maps, photographs, and newspapers

1200 S.W. Park Avenue
Portland, OR 97205-2483
Telephone: 503-222-1741
Fax: 503-221-2035
E-mail: orhist@ohs.org

The Oregon Historical Society: http://www.ohs.org/

Oregon Genealogical Society - Donation land claims, Oregon cemetery records, Oregon death indexes, periodicals, pedigree charts

955 Oak Alley
Eugene, OR 97401-3148
Tel: (541) 345-0399

Oregon Genealogical Society:
http://www.oregongenealogicalsociety.org/

Oregon Mailing Lists

Mailing lists are internet based facilities that use email to distribute a single message to all who subscribe to it. When information on a particular surname, new records, or any other important genealogy information related to the mailing list topic becomes available, the subscribers are alerted to it. Joining a mailing list is an excellent way to stay up to date on Oregon genealogy research topics. Rootsweb have an extensive listing of **Oregon Mailing Lists** on a variety of topics.

Oregon Mailing Lists:
http://lists.rootsweb.ancestry.com/index/usa/OR/misc.html

Oregon Message Boards

A message board is another internet based facility where people can post questions about a specific genealogy topic and have it answered by other genealogists. If you have questions about a surname, record type, or research topic, you can post your question and other researchers and genealogists will help you with the answer. Be sure to check back regularly, as the answers are not emailed to you. The Oregon message boards at **Rootsweb** are completely free to use.

Rootsweb:
http://boards.rootsweb.com/localities.northam.usa.states/mb.ashx

Oregon Newspapers and Periodicals

Many genealogy periodicals and historical newspapers contain reprinted copies of family genealogies, transcripts of family Bible records, information about local records and archives, census indexes, church records, queries, land records, obituaries, court records, cemetery records, and wills. The following sites have historical Oregon newspapers and periodicals that you can search online or on-site.

The Oregon Historical Society – large variety of historical Oregon newspapers

1200 S.W. Park Avenue
Portland, OR 97205-2483
Telephone: 503-222-1741
Fax: 503-221-2035
E-mail: orhist@ohs.org

The Oregon Historical Society: http://www.ohs.org/

GenealogyBank.com – free searchable database of Oregon newspaper archives, 1850-1987

GenealogyBank.com:
http://www.genealogybank.com/gbnk/newspapers/explore/USA/Oregona/

The Online Books Page – links to historical Oregon books and periodicals available for viewing online

The Online Books Page: http://onlinebooks.library.upenn.edu

Library of Congress Digital Newspaper Directory – free searchable database of historical U.S. newspapers dating from 1690-present

Library of Congress Digital Newspaper Directory:
http://chroniclingamerica.loc.gov/search/titles/

NewspaperArchive.com – largest online database of historical newspapers in the world.

NewspaperArchive.com: http://newspaperarchive.com/

Historical Oregon Maps and Gazetteers

Maps are an integral part of genealogical research. They help us to locate landmarks, towns, cities, parishes, states, provinces, waterways and roads and streets. They also help us to determine when and where boundary changes might have taken place, and give us a visualization of the area we're researching in.

For locating place names, a gazetteer is the best possible resource for any genealogist. Gazetteers are also sometimes called "place name dictionaries", and can help you to locate the area in which you need to conduct research. Below are links to the maps and gazetteers for research in Oregon.

Peabody GNIS Service – Oregon:
http://peabody.research.yale.edu/cgi-bin/Query.GNIS?ST=Oregon&SU=1

Color Landform Atlas – Oregon:
http://fermi.jhuapl.edu/states/or_0.html

1985 U.S. Atlas: http://www.livgenmi.com/1895/OR/

Oregon Hometown Locator: http://oregon.hometownlocator.com/

<u>Oregon City Directories</u>

.

City directories are similar to telephone directories in that they list the residents of a particular area. The difference though is what is important to genealogists, and that is they pre-date telephone directories. You can find an ancestor's information such as their street address, place of employment, occupation, or the name of their spouse. A one-stop-shop for finding city directories in Oregon is the **Oregon Online Historical Directories** which contains a listing of every available online historical directory related to Oregon.

Oregon Online Historical Directories:
https://sites.google.com/site/onlinedirectorysite/Home/usa/or

The Oregon Historical Society – variety of Oregon city directories listing an individual's address, occupation, and spouse

1200 S.W. Park Avenue
Portland, OR 97205-2483
Telephone: 503-222-1741
Fax: 503-221-2035
E-mail: orhist@ohs.org

The Oregon Historical Society: http://www.ohs.org/

Oregon Genealogical Records

<u>Birth, Death, Marriage and Divorce Records</u> – Also known as vital records, birth, death, and marriage certificates are the most basic, yet most important records attached to your ancestor. The reason for their importance is that they not only place your ancestor in a specific place at a definite time, but potentially connect the individual to other relatives. Below is a list of repositories and websites where you can find Oregon vital records.

The Center for Health Statistics - birth and death records dating from 1903; marriage records from 1906; and divorce certificates (not decrees) from 1925.

800 NE Oregon Street, Suite 205
Portland, OR 97232
Tel: 1-888-896-4988

Mailing Address:

Oregon Vital Records
PO Box 14050
Portland OR 97293

The Center for Health Statistics:
http://public.health.oregon.gov/BirthDeathCertificates/GetVitalReco
rds/Pages/index.aspx

Oregon State Archives – Huge database of city, county, and state divorce, marriage, birth, and death records and indexes dating from 1850's to present

800 Summer St. NE
Salem OR 97310
Tel:503-373-0701
Fax 503-373-0953

Oregon State Archives:
http://sos.oregon.gov/archives/Pages/records.aspx

Family Search has the following indexes which can be searched online for free:

Oregon, Births and Christenings, 1868-1929:
https://familysearch.org/search/collection/1675468

Oregon, County Marriages, 1851-1975:
https://familysearch.org/search/collection/1803968

Oregon, Death Index, 1903-1998:
https://familysearch.org/search/collection/1946790

Oregon, Deaths and Burials, 1903-1947:
https://familysearch.org/search/collection/1675532

Oregon, Marriages, 1853-1935:
https://familysearch.org/search/collection/1675533

Census Reports

Census records are among the most important genealogical documents for placing your ancestor in a particular place at a specific time. Like BDM records, they can also lead you to other ancestors, particularly those who were living under the authority of the head of household.

Federal census records for Oregon exist from 1860 –1930 and can be found at:

Oregon State Archives - census records from the provisional, territorial, state and federal governments, Bureau of Indian Affairs census records

800 Summer St. NE
Salem OR 97310
Tel:503-373-0701
Fax 503-373-0953

Oregon State Archives:
http://sos.oregon.gov/archives/Pages/records.aspx

University of Oregon Libraries – Federal, State, and Territorial census records dating from 1860-1930

1501 Kincaid Street,
Eugene, OR 97403-1299
Tel: (541) 346-3053
Fax: (541) 346-3485

University of Oregon Libraries:
http://library.uoregon.edu/guides/genealogy/index.html

The Oregon Historical Society – Provisional and Territorial Government Census records for the years 1842 – 1859, the research library has the United States Federal Census for the years 1850, 1860, 1870, 1880, 1900, 1910, 1920, and 1930

1200 S.W. Park Avenue
Portland, OR 97205-2483
Telephone: 503-222-1741
Fax: 503-221-2035
E-mail: **orhist@ohs.org**

The Oregon Historical Society: http://www.ohs.org/

National Archives – Federal census Schedules for all states, 1790-1940

8601 Adelphi Road
College Park, MD 20740-6001
Tel: 1-866-272-6272

National Archives: http://www.archives.gov/research/census/

The **Free Census Project** has transcribed many Oregon indexes and new material is added daily

Free Census Project: http://usgwcensus.org/cenfiles/or.htm

Access Genealogy – Oregon county census records dating from 1860-1930

Access Genealogy:
http://www.accessgenealogy.com/census/oregon-census-records.htm

African American Census Schedules Online – slave schedules, mortality schedules, slave-owners census

African American Census Schedules Online:
http://www.afrigeneas.com/aacensus/

Native Americans in Census Records (US National Archives): http://www.archives.gov/research/census/native-americans/

Oregon Church Records

Church and synagogue records are a valuable resource, especially for baptisms, marriages, and burials that took place before 1900. You will need to at least have an idea of your ancestor's religious denomination, and in most cases you will have to visit a brick and mortar establishment to view them.

Most church records are kept by the individual church, although in some denominations, records are placed in a regional archive or maintained at the diocesan level. Local Historical Societies are sometimes the repository for the state's older church records. Below are links archives that maintain church records, as well as a few databases that can be viewed online.

The **Family History Library** contains many church records from a variety of denominations on microfilm.

Family History Library:
http://familysearch.org/learn/wiki/en/Family_History_Library

Central Repositories for Denominational Records

Church of Jesus Christ of Latter-day Saints (Mormons)

Early Mormon Church records for Oregon can be found on film located at the LDS Family History Library in Salt Lake City and can be searched via the **Family History Library Catalog**

Family History Library Catalog:
https://familysearch.org/eng/Library/FHLC/frameset_fhlc.asp

Baptist

Southern Baptist Convention
901 Commerce Street #400
Nashville, TN 37203-3699
Phone: (615) 244-0344
Fax: (615) 782-4821

Southern Baptist Convention: http://www.sbhla.org/

Disciples of Christ

Disciples of Christ Historical Society
1101 Nineteenth Avenue, South
Nashville, TN 37212
Phone: (615) 327-1444
Fax: (615) 327-1445

Disciples of Christ Historical Society:
http://www.discipleshistory.org/

Methodist

United Methodist Church Archives
P.O. Box 127 Drew University
36 Madison Ave.
Madison, NJ 07940-3189
Telephone: 973-408-3189
Fax: 973-408-3909
E-mail: research@gcah.org

United Methodist Church Archives:
http://www.gcah.org/site/c.ghKJI0PHIoE/b.2858857/k.BF4D/Home.
htm

Presbyterian

Presbytery of the Cascades
Northeast/Northwest Office
0245 S.W. Bancroft Street, Suite D
Portland, OR 97239-4272
Phone: 800-495-4114
Local: 503-227-5486
Fax: 503-227-6045

Presbytery of the Cascades: http://www.cascadespresbytery.org/

Presbytery of Eastern Oregon
1358 SW Eleventh Street
Ontario, OR 97914
Phone: 541-889-5592

Presbytery of Eastern Oregon:
http://www.pbyofeasternoregon.org/

Society of Friends (Quakers)

George Fox College
Quaker Collection
414 N. Meridian Street
Newberg, OR 97132-2697
Phone: (503) 538-8383

George Fox College: http://www.georgefox.edu/

<u>Roman Catholic</u>

Archdiocese of Portland in Oregon
Chancery Office
2838 E. Burnside Street
Portland, OR 97214-1895
Phone: (503) 234-5334
Fax: (503) 234-2545

Mailing address:
P.O. Box 351
Portland, OR 97214-1895

Archdiocese of Portland in Oregon:
http://www.archdpdx.org/archives/

Oregon Military Records

More than 40 million Americans have participated in some time of war service since America was colonized. The chance of finding your ancestor amongst those records is exceptionally high. Military records can even reveal individuals who never actually served, such as those who registered for the two World Wars but were never called to duty.

Below are a number of links to websites and archives that contain Oregon military records.

Oregon State Archives - Correspondences, Reports, Public relations releases, Claim files, Minutes, Bonds, Election returns, Enlistment and service records, Medical case records, Legal case records, Muster rolls, Rosters, Logs and Applications

800 Summer St. NE
Salem OR 97310
Tel:503-373-0701
Fax 503-373-0953

Oregon State Archives:
http://sos.oregon.gov/archives/Pages/records.aspx

The Oregon Historical Society –Indian Wars Pensions Index, DAR Index

1200 S.W. Park Avenue
Portland, OR 97205-2483
Telephone: 503-222-1741
Fax: 503-221-2035
E-mail: orhist@ohs.org

The Oregon Historical Society: http://www.ohs.org/

US Department of Veterans Affairs Nationwide Gravesite Locator – includes information on veterans and their family members buried in veterans and military cemeteries having a government grave marker.

US Department of Veterans Affairs Nationwide Gravesite Locator: http://gravelocator.cem.va.gov/

You may also find your ancestor's military records in the following databases:

United States General Index to Pension Files, 1861-1934: https://familysearch.org/search/collection/1919699

United States Index to Service Records, War with Spain, 1898: https://familysearch.org/search/collection/1919583

United States Index to Indian Wars Pension Files, 1892-1926 – military pension records of soldiers who fought in the Indian Wars between 1817 and 1898

United States Index to Indian Wars Pension Files, 1892-1926: https://familysearch.org/search/collection/1979427

United States Registers of Enlistments in the U.S. Army, 1798-1914 - index of men who enlisted in the United States Army, 1798-1914.

United States Registers of Enlistments in the U.S. Army, 1798-1914: https://familysearch.org/search/collection/1880762

United States Mexican War Pension Index, 1887-1926 link to: https://familysearch.org/search/collection/1979390

Civil War Soldiers Service Records - Service records for both Union and Confederate soldiers indexed by soldier's name, rank, and unit.

Civil War Soldier Service Records: http://go.fold3.com/civilwar_records/

Oregon Cemetery Records

As convenient as it is to search cemetery records online, keep in mind that there are a few disadvantages over visiting a cemetery in person. They are:

- Tombstone information is not always accurately transcribed
- The arrangement of the graves in a cemetery can be crucial as family members are often buried next to each other or in the same grave. This arrangement is not always preserved in the alphabetical indexes that are found online.

With that information in mind, the following websites have databases that can be searched online for Oregon Cemetery records.

Oregon Genealogical Society – large collection of county cemetery records from around the state

955 Oak Alley
Eugene, OR 97401-3148
Tel: (541) 345-0399

Oregon Genealogical Society:
http://www.oregongenealogicalsociety.org/

Oregon Tombstone Transcription Project - death and burial records

Oregon Tombstone Transcription Project:
http://usgwtombstones.org/oregon/oregon.html

African American Cemeteries Online – African American, slave, and Native American cemetery records

African American Cemeteries Online:
http://africanamericancemeteries.com/

Access Genealogy – database of Oregon cemetery record transcriptions

Access Genealogy:
http://www.accessgenealogy.com/cemetery/oregon-cemetery-records.htm

Find a Grave – over 100 million grave records can be searched on this site. Search can be conducted by name, location, or cemetery name.

Find a Grave: http://www.findagrave.com/

Interment.net - A free online database containing approximately 4 million cemetery records from around the world.

Interment.net: http://www.interment.net/

Billion Graves – as the name implies, you can search a billion records including headstone photos, transcriptions, cemetery records, and grave locations.

Billion Graves:
http://billiongraves.com/pages/search/index.php#cemetery

Oregon Obituaries

Obituaries can reveal a wealth about our ancestor and other relatives. You can search our **Oregon Obituaries Listings** from hundreds of Oregon newspapers online for free.

Oregon Obituaries Listings:
http://obituarieshelp.org/oregon_newspaper_obituaries.html

Oregon Wills and Probate Records

The documents found in a probate packet may include a complete inventory of a person's estate, newspaper entries, witness testimony, a copy of a will, list of debtors and creditors, names of executors or trustees, names of heirs. They can not only tell you about the ancestor you're currently researching, but lead to other ancestors.

Probate records in Oregon were kept in **Oregon County Courts** from the time of each county's creation.

Oregon County Courts:
http://courts.oregon.gov/OJD/courts/pages/index.aspx

You may also find Oregon Probate records at:

Oregon State Archives - Probate Bond Registers, Letters of Administration, Case Files, Dower Records, Estate Records, Guardianship Records, Letters of Testamentary, Probate Orders, and many more probate related documents dating from 1840's to late 1900's
800 Summer St. NE
Salem OR 97310
Tel:503-373-0701
Fax 503-373-0953

Oregon State Archives:
http://sos.oregon.gov/archives/Pages/records.aspx

Family Search has the following online indexes which can be searched for free:

Oregon, Benton County Records:
https://familysearch.org/search/collection/1929994

Oregon, Polk County Records:
https://familysearch.org/search/collection/1453591

Oregon Immigration and Naturalization Records

The naturalization process generated many types of records, including petitions, declarations of intention, and oaths of allegiance. These records can provide family historians with information such as a person's birth date and place of birth, immigration year, marital status, spouse information, occupation, witnesses' names and addresses, and more.

Oregon State Archives - Citizen Certificates, Naturalization Declarations of Intention, Naturalization Petitions & Records, Naturalization Certificates, Naturalization Citizenship Applications, Naturalization Petitions, and many other related records dating from 1850's to late 20th century

800 Summer St. NE
Salem OR 97310
Tel:503-373-0701
Fax 503-373-0953

Oregon State Archives:
http://sos.oregon.gov/archives/Pages/records.aspx

University of Oregon Libraries - Applications to Immigrant and Naturalization Service, documentations of requests for visa extensions, related documentation and correspondence including letters of support

1501 Kincaid Street,
Eugene, OR 97403-1299
Tel: (541) 346-3053
Fax: (541) 346-3485

University of Oregon Libraries:
http://library.uoregon.edu/guides/genealogy/index.html

Oregon Native American Records

National Archives—Pacific Alaska Region (Seattle) - records relating to the Five Civilized Tribes

6125 Sand Point Way, N.E.
Seattle, WA 98115-7999
Telephone: 206-336-5115
Fax: 206-336-5112

National Archives—Pacific Alaska Region (Seattle):
http://www.archives.gov/seattle/

Access Genealogy – Oregon Native American census records, tribal histories, and much more:
http://www.accessgenealogy.com/native/oregon-indian-tribes.htm

U.S. National Archives - information on American Indians who maintained their ties to Federally-recognized Tribes (1830-1970).

U.S. National Archives: http://www.archives.gov/research/native-americans/

Records of the Bureau of Indian Affairs (BIA):
http://www.archives.gov/research/guide-fed-records/groups/075.html

American Indians Records Repository - records dating from the 1700s including trust, education and other historic Indian Affairs records

American Indian Records Repository
Meritex Enterprises
17501 West 98th Street
Lenexa, KS 66219
Phone: 913-888-0601

American Indians Records Repository:
http://www.doi.gov/ost/records_mgmt/american-indian-records-repository.cfm

Missing Matriarchs – Resources for Researching Female Oregon Ancestors

Looking for female ancestors requires an adjustment of how we view traditional records sources. A woman's identity was often under that of her husband, and often individual records for them can be difficult to locate. The following resources are effective in locating female ancestors in Oregon where traditional records may not reveal them.

Bibliographies

1. *Northwest Women: An Annotated Bibliography of Sources on the History of Oregon and Washington Women, 1787-1970,* Karen J. Blair (Washington State University Press, 1976)
2. *Women's Voices From the Oregon Trail: The Times that Tried Women's Souls and a Guide to Women's History Along the Oregon Trail,* Patricia Brandt and Kathleen Petersen (Tamarack Books, 1994)
3. *Treasures in the Trunk: Quilts of the Oregon Trail,* Mary Bywater Cross (Rutledge Hill Press, 1993)
4. *Select Bibliography of Women's Studies: Holdings of the Women's Center Library at Oregon State University,* Judith A. Glenn (Oregon State University Press, 1988)
5. *Covered Wagon Women: Diaries and Letters From the Western Trails, 1852: The Oregon Trail,* Kenneth L. Holmes (University of Nebraska Press, 1997)

Selected Resources for Oregon Women's History

Center Oregon
CommunityCollege Library
NW College Way
Bend, OR 97701

Oregon Historical Society
1200 SW Park Avenue
Portland, OR 97205

Women's Center Library
Oregon State University
Corvallis, OR 97333

Common Oregon Surnames

The following surnames are among the most common in Oregon and are also being currently researched by other genealogists. If you find your surname here, there is a chance that some research has already been performed on your ancestor.

Alexander, Alfart, Andrey, Anna, Ball, Barnes, Brock, Broer, Broers, Bryant, Buessenschuett, Carson, Cole, Copenhaver, Cox, Cranmer, Descloux, Dinwiddie, Downs, Elizabeth, Eoff, Euchler, Fannin, Findley, Frances, Gray, Gsuiter, Hainey, Hamilton, Hannah, Hansen, Harris, Hitchman, Hohimer, Holland, Hope, Jones, Jr., Julia, Kleemeyer, Klemeyer, Koehler, Koster, Mains, Margaret, Mary, McGray, McKinzie, Means, Meier, Moore, Morton, Nation, Nussbaum, Ogle, Pack, Paine, Parsons, Potter, Robbins, Robertson, Robins, Robinson, Sally, Schierloh, Schmeckpeper, Sebade, Seebade, Shirtz, Spanheimer, Stagler, Stephenson, Suiter, Susan, Thomas, Vickery, Wade, Warneke, Weissenfluh, Wells, Wilson, Wollaston, Yeureth

About the Author

Gary L. Morris worked from 2009 to 2014 as a professional researcher for a major player in the genealogy field. After tracing his family lineage back to 1683, he found that genealogy could be an expensive undertaking. As such, has decided to publish these helpful guides to share the valuable free information he has discovered during his career to help others trace their family lineages as inexpensively as possible. An avid genealogist himself, he hopes you will find this guide factual, thorough, helpful, and most of all, effective in helping you to find your family members.

Notes

Notes